The uncolored father: interracial bathhouse tales

By:Anthony Hawkins

ISBN:978-1-312-31095-7

Dedicated to the gay and lesbian community.

Prologue

Ray was a 25 year old black male who lived with his 35 year old caucasian adopted father Sam,Sam adopting Ray so that Ray could inherit his belongings and property one day.

Sam had met Ray on a street corner near a local gay bar he attended occasionally,he and Ray then becoming good friends as they got closer and closer,Sam taking Ray in and even placing Ray's name on his lease,Sam wanting Ray to have a place to stay and a bit of financial assistance.

Neither Ray nor Sam had many close relatives,all they had was each other,and they didn't mind it.

Sam's main purpose of adopting Ray was because he had saw that Ray had slightly struggled financially,and he wanted to make sure that Ray would be better taken care of in the future,Ray now excelling financially and professionally.

Ray and Sam's relationship grew and grew over time,and they did almost everything together,they camped together,they exercised and lifted weights together,and they even watched movies together from time to time.

Sam and Ray's relationship intensified once they discovered that they were both same sex oriented,their connection becoming stronger.

Chapter 1

It was a friday afternoon and both Ray and Sam were working out together,their hands lifting weights as they flexed and exercised,both their bodies dressed in a tank top and a pair of sweat pants,perspiration rolling down their toned bodies from their intense workout.

You building a little muscle over there,Sam complimented Ray on his physique.Thank's man,you looking buff yourself,Ray complimented Sam as well.

Thats enough for today dude,wanna hit the showers? Sam spoke to Ray as he stood tall to his feet.Yea,im cool with that,Ray spoke to Sam as he gently placed the weights in his hands to the floor of the excercise room.

Ray and Sam then headed to the shower room together as they peeled themselves out of all of their clothes,Ray and Sam both entering a shower stall as their hands twisted the showerheads on,the hot raining showerheads beating down on their naked bodies.

Ray and Sam were both handsome and attractive men,Ray having smooth chocolate brown colored skin and white teeth,full lips,dark and thick hair,and a toned body,and Sam having smooth peachy golden and slightly bronze colored skin with smooth pink lips and an exotic look to him,his hair dark and full,and his voice deep and dense.

How's school been going? Sam questioned Ray as they both showered next to each other.It's been cool,same old,same old,you know,Ray spoke to Sam.Cool,Sam spoke back to Ray.I was thinking maybe we could go up to the mountains next weekend for some father and son time,if thats cool with you? Sam spoke to Ray.It's all good,we can do that,Ray spoke to Sam as he soaped his nude body.

Ray and Sam soaped and washed themselves thoroughly under the hot raining showerheads as the showerheads rained down on their naked bodies heavily.

Chapter 2

Ray and Sam then rinsed themselves off one last time and then turned off the showerheads after they were done with their steamy hot showers.

Ray and Sam stepped themselves out of the shower stalls as they tightly placed short white above knee length towels around the waists of their tall naked toned and sculpted bodies,their damp feet sliding into shower shoes and flip flops.

That shower was sweet man,Sam spoke to Ray as they both exited the shower room and into the long hall of their home side by side in nothing but the short white towels around their naked waists,their shower shoes and flip flops lightly thumping against the hardwood floor as they headed down the hall.

Wanna watch some porn man? Sam questioned Ray as they entered the living area.Cool,Ray spoke to Sam smoothly.

Ray and Sam both gave each other a silent glance of guilty intrigue as they examined each others handsome faces,and then each others wide and broad shoulders,and then each others long and muscled arms,and then each others smooth and firm pecks,and then each others smooth and toned abs,and then each others strong and smooth and long thighs and knees and legs that protruded from the short white above knee length towels around the naked waists of their naked bodies.

Sam stared at Ray for a little while longer and then kissed Ray gently on the lips as Ray kissed him back softly.My bad dude,im supposed to be like a father to you,we cant do this,Sam spoke silently to Ray as their lips departed slowly and hesitantly.

Ray ignored Sam's words as he began to kiss Sam,Sam then kissing him back in deep lust as their kiss became more intense and provocative and passionate,their tongues meeting as their toned chests met,their abs touching,the fabric of their short white above knee length towels grazing,their long strong thighs and knees and legs mingling,and their shower shoes and flip flops clashing.

Ray and Sam then began to grope and fondle each other lustfully as they continued to passionately kiss.

Let's have some father and son experimentation man,i wanna make love to you,it'll be our way of bonding,Sam spoke silently to Ray in a moan,Ray agreeing,both of them in a state of arousal.

Sam placed himself and Ray to the cushions of the living area sofa as he towered himself over Ray gently,he and Ray's lips meeting as their chests and towel covered crotch areas and thighs and knees met softly.Sam then pulled the towel from the waist of his hard and muscled naked body as he gently unwrapped Ray's towel from the waist of his toned and sculpted naked body as well,the naked flesh of their bodies colliding.

Sam then lubed himself as he smoothly glided himself into Ray in a gasp of his smooth and kissable lips,Sam and Ray's naked bodies fleshly connecting in thrill.Sam then began to moved himself up and down on top of Ray's nude body in a smooth jerky grinding rhythm of his nude body as Ray began to moan out in pleasure.

Ray and Sam's naked bodies jerked back and forth on the sofa as they both moaned out in pleasure,the pleasure of their hot naked flesh connecting and colliding giving them intense thrills of sexual pleasure and energy.

Sam's round and hard buttocks flexed and jerked as he continued to plunge himself inbetween Ray's tight fleshly tunnel in their nudity,their eyes staring lustfully and intimately at each other as they rocked back and forth heavily in lust,passion,and pleasure,Ray's inner loins deeply throbbing and heating in pleasure and near orgasmic thrills.

Sam's exposed crotch began to thrust closely and smoothly onto Ray's as their pelvises met in the friction of their hot and naked sexual encounter,both their bodies entangled in a pit of their hot and naked flesh as the sound of moans and meeting flesh whisked across the room.

Im gonna cum! Sam moaned out to Ray as he trembled in lust and ecstasy,his face giving away his pleasure.

Sam then shoved himself a few more times into Ray and then quickly and smoothly pulled himself from Ray as his strong muscular thighs clenched to Ray's strong and sculpted hips as the muscles of his sculpted body flexed and then his huge penis ejaculating hot and thick semen all over Ray's toned naked body and abs as Ray reached an orgasm as well,Ray feeling himself reach an intense explosion of passion and sexual peak as he and Sam moaned and whimpered in intense pleasure of their taboo naked adopted father and naked adopted son sexual kicks.

Sam spanked Ray's naked body with his exposed thick shaft and huge and plump mushroom tip hard penis as his own naked body flexed and trembled lightly above Ray's,Sam massaging his warm semen onto Ray's exposed crotch as Ray laid beneath him in excitement.

Sam and Ray's lips met once again as Sam laid his smooth and naked peachy golden bronze colored body onto Ray's smooth and naked chocolate brown colored body,their lips making impact as did their hot nudity,their towels dangling over the used and abused sofa.

Ray and Sam's adopted father and adopted son relationship had grown more intimate and sexual and romantic in nature,and they embraced it with guilty pleasure.

The end

Moms black son & Moms white boss (bathhouse tale)

By:Anthony Hawkins

Dedicated to the gay and lesbian community.

Prologue

Jamal was a young handsome 27 year old black male with smooth chocolate brown colored skin and bright white teeth that gleamed through his full and smooth lips,he had pecks that bulged,abs that were smooth and visible,thighs and legs that were strong and toned,and arms that were muscular but not overdone,his hair dark and thick,and his shoulders wide,his voice smooth and slightly deep.

Tho Jamal had money and a decent life he still longed for more.

Jamal still struggled to tell his family about his same sex orientation,Jamal feeling that his family would disown and ostrasize him for it,Jamal's family had no clue that he was same sex oriented,they had no clue that he had dated other men on and off discreetly,they had no clue that he visited gay nightclubs and gay bathhouses from time to time,they knew nothing at all of his personal life,only that he was a loving relative who would sometimes seem out of place and bothered.

Chapter 1

It was a friday night,and Jamal was sitting home on his sofa watching his television set silently,his cellphone then ringing from inside his shirt pocket,the sounds of the ringing phone startling him.

Hello? Jamal answered his cellphone quickly and smoothly.Hey baby,this your mama,im just calling to see how you doing,you been alright,haven't heard from you in awhile? A woman spoke to Jamal through the phone,the woman being Jamal's mother.

I been alright,just been a little tired lately,that's about it tho,Jamal spoke to the woman,yarning a bit afterwards.Oh ok,good to hear baby,look,your aunt Gloria got a nice young girl she want you to meet next week,Jamal's mother spoke to Jamal,a smile in her voice.

Naw ma,im a little busy next week,but tell aunt Gloria i said hi,Jamal spoke to his mother,slight annoyance in his voice.Boy when are you going to settle down and meet a nice girl,aint you getting lonely up in that house of yours? Jamal's mother questioned him with concern.

Im good being alone ma,i aint got time for no female right now,i like being lonely,i aint got nobody to answer to,but anyway,i love you ma,i gotta go,i call you a little later alright,Jamal spoke to his mother.Alright,i talk to you later then,im having lunch with my boss tomorrow afternoon anyway,he a nice young man,he kind of remind me of you in some ways in character,except he white,he aint got no girlfriend or wife either,they call him a bachelor at work,but anyway,need to get my sleep,love you too,bye baby,Jamal's mother ended her and jamal's call,Jamal then placing his cellphone back into his shirt pocket after he and his mothers call ended.

Jamal stood to his feet as he checked the time on his clock,Jamal then getting himself fully dressed as he turned off his televison set with a tv remote.Jamal shrugged into a thin jacket as he grabbed his keys from off of his dining room table.Jamal then headed out of the front door of his house,locking up after exiting.

Jamal headed to a secluded bathhouse at the far edge of town near the woods to relax,Jamal parking his car near a tree and then heading inside of the bathhouse by himself.

Jamal headed into a silent and unoccupied room of the bathhouse and then began to undress himself,shrugging out of all his clothes until he was standing completely naked.

Jamal then headed into one of the private shower rooms where he showered himself under the raining showerhead,the hot water heavily beating down against his naked flesh as he soaped himself up,and then rinsing himself off.

Chapter 2

Jamal showered himself for thirty minutes and then finally headed out of the shower room as he pulled a short white towel around the waist of his naked toned body,his feet sliding into shower shoes.

Jamal headed down one of the huge halls of the bathhouse in nothing but the short and skimpy white towel around his waist and the shower shoes on his feet as he passed the provocative male sounds of pleasure within some of the private rooms he passed by,Jamal then accidently bumping into an attractive caucasian male on his way down the hall.

Oh,my bad man,Jamal quickly apologized to the caucasian male,his face apologetic.No problem dude,i should have watched where i was going,my bad too,the man spoke warmly and politely to jamal,his warm caramel colored eyes staring into Jamal's dark brown eyes,a short white towel around his naked waist as well,flip flops on his feet.

You come here often? the caucasian man questioned Jamal with curiosity,his face smooth,shaven,and hairless,his hair neatly cut short dark straight full and shiny,his smooth and kissable pink lips almost as full as Jamal's,his voice just as deep as Jamal's,with well spoken grammer to go along.Naw,not really,i come here every now and then,just to relax,Jamal explained to the caramel colored eyed man.Nice bumping into you dude,i see you around,Jamal then walked away from the caucasian male.Nice bumping into you too,the man spoke to Jamal as he and Jamal both parted ways.

Jamal headed into a secluded corner of the bathhouse and then stood to the wall silently as he relaxed to himself,his eyes watching a fountain near one of the private rooms.Jamal saw the caucasian male he had previously ran into resting against a wall as well,their eyes meeting every now and then.

The caucasion male gave Jamal one last glance and then began to head over to him smoothly.I dont mean to pry,but are you here alone man? the caucasion male questioned Jamal as he reached him.Yea,pretty much dude,i like chilling to myself sometimes,Jamal spoke to the man.So,you got a boyfriend or something dude,or are you single? the caucasian man questioned Jamal.Naw,aint got one of those,just doing me right now,what about you? Jamal spoke to the man.Nah,but i do wanna get back out there and start dating again,i broke up with my ex a few months ago,but now that im over him i wanna start dating again,a man gets lonely after awhile you know,the man explained to Jamal as they stared eye to eye.I feel you dude,i aint going lie,i get lonely every now and then too,Jamal admitted to the man in a sincere tone of voice.

Jamal and the caucasian man stared at each other from top to bottom with desire,the caucasian male studying Jamal's sculpted body,starting with Jamal's bulging supple pecks,and then Jamal's smooth abs,and then Jamal's strong and toned legs that protruded from the short white towel around Jamal's waist.Jamal stared at the caucasian mans toned body as well,Jamal starting with the mans firm pecks and

and smooth toned abs,and then the mans strong and lean legs that darted from the short above knee length white towel around his waist as well.

So,dude you wanna go into a private room and talk,kind of chilly out here,and us being only in these towels isn't helping matters,you wanna come with? the caucasian male spoke to Jamal suavely,his eyes warm and welcoming.Yea,cool,we can do that,Jamal spoke to the man,Jamal deciding to go along with him.What's your name by the way man? the caucasian man questioned Jamal.

My name Jamal,you can call me Mal,or just Jamal,Jamal spoke to the man.Cool,my name is Aidan,some people call me Dan for short tho,the caucasian man smiled warmly at Jamal as they began to head down the hallway.Cool,nice meeting you then Aidan,Jamal smiled back at Aidan.Thank's dude,nice meeting you too,Aidan spoke to Jamal.

Jamal and Aidan headed down the marble floor hallway of the bathhouse in only the short white towels around the waists of their toned naked bodies and the shower shoes and flip flops on their feet as they searched for an empty private room.

Here we go,here's an empty room,let's go in shall we,Aidan spoke to Jamal as he let Jamal enter the room first,and then entering himself inside the room behind him,shutting the door behind them.

Gay adult pornagraphy played on the small flat screen tv inside the private room Jamal and Aidan entered,Aidan then turning off the tv as he and Jamal silently stared at each other.Jamal bit his lip gently as he and Aidan continued to stare eye to eye,Jamal's heartbeat beginning to race.Dont take this the wrong way man,but you're fucking hot dude,i have to admit,Aidan spoke seductively to Jamal,his eyes examining Jamal's body.Thank's man,you not so bad yourself,you an attractive dude,Jamal spoke back to Aidan smoothly,his eyes on every part of Aidan.

Would you get mad if i kissed you dude? Aidan questioned Jamal silently and smoothly.Naw,it's cool,Jamal answered Aidan's question,inviting Aidan to kiss him.Aidan moved closer to Jamal and then began to kiss him softly on the lips,their lips locking again and again.

Jamal and Aidan stood lip to lip,chest to chest,towel to towel,thigh to thigh,knee to knee,smooth Chocolate brown colored skin to smooth peachy vanilla cream colored skin as they embraced in an intimate and passionate and lustful kiss.

Jamal and Aidan's tongues met as they continued to kiss,their lips colliding more ferociously as their pulses began to race rapidly,both Jamal and Aidan in a trance of lust.

Jamal grabbed the back of Aidan's head,rushing his lips onto Aidan's before Aidan's could reach his again,Jamal and Aidan trembling and moaning subtly as they kissed passionately.Pull out that hard cock dude,fuck yea,Aidan murmured to jamal as he reached his hand underneath jamal's towel,getting a handful of Jamal's male genitals.

Aidan began to stroke Jamal's hardening penis,massaging it back and forth as he stroked himself as well.Can i blow that hard black dick of yours dude? Aidan moaned silently to Jamal as Jamal moaned out in agreement.Yea,suck that shit man,Jamal moaned out to Aidan as he chucked his huge slinky penis into his hand,waiting for Aidan's mouth to meet with it.

Aidan kneeled to his knees and then slowly placed the tip of Jamal's penis into his wet and warm mouth as he stroked himself from under his towel.Aidan's head began to move back and forth on Jamal's penis as Jamal whimpered in pleasure.Aidan began to lick the shaft and mushroom shaped tip of Jamal's penis with his tongue,giving the head a tease before shoving it back into his mouth,Aidan then gulping and devouring it whole in a deep intense throating action.

The private room was filled with Jamal's moans and the slurping and popping sounds of jamal and Aidan's oral sex.Jamal's hand guided Aidan's head quickly up and down on his erect penis in a fast pace as he dropped his towel to the floor from the waist of his toned naked body,Jamal's hand holding tightly to the back of Aidan's skull.

Aidan began to suck and chokingly gurgle on Jamal's penis with even more intense friction of his bobbing head as Jamal's penis began to throb

violently.Take it out your mouth nigga,im about to bust one! Jamal shouted out to Aidan as he tried to remove Aidan's mouth from his deeply throbbing penis.Aidan ignored Jamal's warning as he pushed Jamal's hand away,still gulping and gagging on Jamal's hard penis until semen erupted from the huge mushroom shaped tip into his waiting mouth,the semen flooding Aidan's warm mouth as Jamal moaned out in deep pleasure from his intense ejaculation in Aidan's mouth.

Fuck man! Jamal yelled in pleasure,feeling himself shoot off

into Aidan's mouth once again.Aidan looked up at Jamal,making eye contact with Jamal's exhausted face.Jamal bit down on his lip gently as he and Aidan made eye contact.Aidan then curved his tongue and mouth around the shaft and head of Jamal's huge penis as he swallowed up the last volcanic eruption of semen that smoothly shot from Jamal's rod as Jamal moaned and groaned in explosive delight.

Nice load man,Aidan smiled at Jamal as he raised from his knees to his feet again,licking his lips smoothly and gently.You can suck a dick man,i gotta

give you your props,Jamal chuckled softly to Aidan.I can do more than that,just meet me here next friday,i'll leave you my number by the front entrance,be sure to look for it dude,im about to leave this place,meeting up with someone tomorrow,Aidan smiled thinly at Jamal as he gave Jamal's now softening penis a gentle squeeze before leaving out the private room,leaving Jamal in the private room to himself.Jamal exhaled one last time in satisfaction and then left the private room.

Jamal thought about his brief sexual encounter with Aidan all throughout the weekend.

Chapter 3

The next week Jamal's mother invited him to visit her at work,Jamal heading to his mothers place of work to visit her,this being his first time visiting her while she was still at work.

May i speak with Corraine Thomas,im here to see her,she's expecting me,im her son Jamal,Jamal spoke politely to a woman at the front desk of his mothers workplace,the woman then making a quick call.

I just informed mrs Thomas that you were here for her,she wants you to come to her office,she's right down the hall to the left,you cant miss her,the woman explained politely to Jamal as Jamal listened to her carefully,and then following her instructions.

Jamal headed to Corraine's office,and then entered silently.Hey,give me a hug,Corraine demanded of Jamal as she hugged him tightly in her arms,a wide smile on her mature and pretty face.

Have a seat,so what's been going on? Corraine spoke to Jamal as she sat back down in her own seat,Jamal then gently sitting down into a chair at her desk afterwards.Aint nothing been going on really,just been living,same old same old,a few new good things been taking place in my life lately tho,Jamal explained to Corraine.

I want you to meet my boss,hold on for just a second,let me call him around,Corraine spoke to Jamal as she placed her office phone to her ears,calling up her boss.

He be right around,just stay patient,Corraine spoke to Jamal after she was done with her call.Jamal and Corraine waited ten minutes for Corraine's boss to arrive,and then eventually he showed up.Hey mr Miller,this is my son Jamal,Jamal this is mr Miller,Corraine introduced her boss and Jamal to one another,a smile on her face.

Jamal spun around in the chair to meet Corraine's boss,but realized he was now staring Aidan directly in the eyes,Aidan staring back at him,both of them in silent shock,slight guilt on their faces.

Aidan and Jamal continued to stay frozen in shock for just a few seconds,but then pretended as if they didn't know each other in front of Jamal's mother Corraine.

Hey,im Aidan,nice to meet you,your mother talks about you all the time,Aidan spoke warmly to Jamal as he shook his hand politely.Nice meeting you too sir,i hear about you from time to time myself,Jamal spoke to Aidan politely,Corraine smiling widely as they conversed.

You have a wonderful son Corraine,but i have to get back to work,and Jamal i hope to see you again,Aidan spoke to Corraine and then Jamal,discreetly caressing Jamal's thigh as he headed out the office,fleeing Jamal and Corraine's sight.

Jamal stayed in the office with Corraine for just a little while longer and then headed out,waving her goodbye as he exited her office.

Jamal then saw Aidan standing silently at the far corner of the room after exiting Corraine's office,Aidan then nodding his head slightly for

Jamal to come over.What's good man? Jamal spoke as he approached Aidan.Im cool man,but i had know idea you were Corraine's son dude? Aidan spoke to Jamal silently.And i didn't know you was my mothers boss,Jamal smirked at Aidan.

Aidan searched the area and then took Jamal back into his office to sneak in a kiss from him,their lips meeting in sparks,their sexual chemistry just as strong as before the first time they met at the bathhouse.You look good in a suit my man,Jamal complimented Aidan on his appearance.Aidan snickered at

Jamal's compliment and then kissed him again softly on the lips.

The days began to pass,and Corraine began to notice a sudden increase in her paycheck,Aidan giving her a raise,something Jamal unintentionally caused by his secret affair with Aidan,Aidan being Jamal's lover and the boss of Jamal's mother.

Chapter 4

It was friday,and Jamal and Aidan had met up together at the secluded bathhouse again,the both of them showering together under one raining showerhead,water cascading down their toned and naked bodies as they continued to shower and kiss,their clothes stuffed into a cupboard of the private room they shared.

Jamal and Aidan pulled short white towels tightly around the waists of their naked bodies after they finished with their hot and steamy shower together,their damp feet stepping into shower shoes and flip flops as they exited the shower stall and into the room area where they began to kiss.

Your mom would probably flip if she knew what we were doing right now dude,Aidan spoke to Jamal as they kissed softly.I feel you,but what mom dont know wont hurt her,Jamal spoke back to Aidan in a silent moan.Jamal and Aidan's lips departed as they heard a knock at the door of the private room they occupied,their affection and romance being disturbed by the knocker.

Who is it? Jamal questioned the knocker as he slowly and lightly swung open the private room door to greet the knocker.It's me,Larry from down the street,i heard that you like to frequent places of these types,but anyway,i wanna speak with you,a stern looking black male spoke to Jamal as he stood outside of the private room Jamal and Aidan shared,his body dressed in dingy blue overalls and a short sleeve undershirt,his skin milky brown and his hair nearly bald.

Yea,what's good man? Jamal spoke to the man Larry with confusion,Jamal secretly wondering why Larry would follow and track him down at the bathhouse.Yea,but anyway,i just wanted to let you know that what you doing aint of God,it aint right for two men to be laying up together,and im not going pretend that it is,this all up in here is sin,the Devil's work,i've seen you come and go time to time,but i just wanted to give you some words of wisdom brotha,Larry spoke to Jamal calmly,Jamal staring at him with a look of discomfort and shock.And then you up in here with a white man my brotha,that's way low,Larry whispered silently to Jamal,not wanting Aidan to hear him,tho Aidan did indeed hear him.

Man im a grown man,i do as i please,im not hurting you or anybody else,this is my life,but thank's for your input anyway dude,but i dont really need it,Jamal spoke to Larry politely,Larry then pausing.Man im just trying help,im trying save another brothas soul man,this here aint nothing but perversion dawg,i dont even wanna be up in here for real,i heard dudes moaning and groaning just as soon as i came in here man,that shit is nasty,i saw black men,white men,latino men,all kinds of men up in here,it's wrong in the Lord's eyes man,Larry explained to

Jamal,Jamal ignoring him as Aidan smoothly stepped up beside him to kiss him passionately in front of Larry,Larry's face nearly going blank in response.

Larry watched in shock as he witnessed Jamal's chocolate colored body and Aidan's peachy vanilla colored body embrace provocatively in a long heated and passion filled kiss as their practically naked bodies groped and embraced in nothing but the short white above knee length towels around their waists in front of his very eyes.

Aidan's eyes peeped over mockingly at Larry's shocked and annoyed face as he and Jamal continued to make out intensely and nearly explicitly before his eyes,Aidan and Jamal hoping Larry got the clear message that they didn't care about his discriminative rants on homosexuality.

He likes it vanilla,Aidan smirked at Larry as he and Jamal continued kissing.And he likes it chocolate,Jamal smirked at Larry as well,Larry then grunting in slight discomfort and anger as he walked away from the black and white kissing pair,both

Jamal and Aidan still kissing as he walked away,and even after he was gone.

Aidan closed and locked the private room door and then eased Jamal onto the cushions of a leather sofa inside the private room as he pulled he and Jamal's short white towels from the waists of their naked bodies,his naked body towering over Jamal's naked body.Aidan lubed himself up,and then gently inserted himself into Jamal as Jamal moaned out softly in response,Jamal's hand latching onto the smooth surface of Aidan's back.Man im in aw dude,i never let a white dude fuck me before,Jamal joked with Aidan as Aidan chuckled silently in response,and then pushing himself a little further into Jamal as Jamal moaned.

Aidan began to thrust his naked body into Jamal's naked body in a sensual rhythm as their bodies rocked together smoothly,Aidan's body moving up and down on Jamal's body as they both experienced lust and pleasure.Aidan began to softly and intimately french kiss Jamal on the lips as they made love in their nudity,Aidan's smooth vanilla peachy colored body colliding with Jamal's smooth chocolate brown body in a swirl pit of their hot naked flesh.

Moans of pleasure escaped Jamal and Aidan's private room as they enjoyed the ecstasy of their sexual intercourse.

Aidan's exposed buttocks flexed as his naked body plunged back and forth into Jamal's naked body,their sex organs throbbing in pleasure.

Jamal's exposed loins began to heat up in throbbing pleasure as he experienced internal pleasure from Aidan's thrusting body,the insanely tight inner walls of Jamal's body hugging tightly to Aidan's exposed penis.Jamal didn't expect Aidan to be well hung and huge down below but he was now receiving the full girth of it smoothly and pleasurably.

Aidan began to push harder into Jamal as he moaned out close to an eruption of sexual release,Jamal's voice vibrating to their naked sexual thrusting action,Jamal's hands gliding up and down Aidan's smooth back and naked buttocks.

Aidan gave Jamal three more thrusts of his hard penis in deep moans of sexual gratification and then quickly

pulled himself out of Jamal as he
ejaculated all over the smooth abs of
Jamal's naked body,Aidan's penis
shooting off thick hot semen from
the smooth and huge mushroom
shaped pale pink head of it in intense
pleasure as Jamal reached a heated
and very pleasurable orgasm of his
own,both Aidan and Jamal moaning
and breathing deeply in deep sexual
pleasure and thrill,Aidan then using
his hard and still shooting penis to
massage and tease Jamal's naked abs
and genitals as Jamal laid beneath
him in ecstasy.

Aidan laid himself on top of Jamal as they kissed,their naked and wet bodies lying against each other in satisfaction as their eyes shut to sleep.

Chapter 5

Jamal and Aidan entered into the shower stall again,where they kissed and touched each other as they soaped up and washed their naked bodies together in lust,the hot raining showerhead sprinkling down on them heavy.

Jamal and Aidan placed short white above knee length towels around the waists of their naked bodies as they exited the shower,and then sliding their feet into shower shoes and flip flops as they headed near the center of the private room.

Jamal stared lustfully at Aidan's very handsome face,and then Aidan's wide and broad shoulders and toned muscled arms,and then Aidan's smooth and supple pecks and toned flat abs,and then Aidan's short white above knee length towel covered waist and crotch area,and then Aidan's smooth long and toned and lean thighs and legs,Aidan watching Jamal's wide and strong shoulders,and Jamal's abs,and Jamal's short white above knee length towel covered waist and crotch,and then Jamal's strong and toned thighs and legs that slightly stood out from the side of his short towel,and then Jamal's huge feet that rested in shower shoes,both Jamal and Aidan watching each other in deep lust.

Jamal rubbed his hand smoothly up the side of Aidan's exposed thigh and short white towel as they stared eye to eye,Aidan touching and squeezing the crotch area of Jamal's short white towel.Jamal then turned Aidan around as he positioned himself behind Aidan,his breath beating down Aidan's smooth and exposed neck and shoulder as Aidan moaned silently at Jamal's warm touch.

Jamal placed Aidan gently to the cushions of the leather sofa and then pulled the short white towel from Aidan's naked waist as Aidan's naked body and buttocks was now on full display to his lustful eyes.Jamal pulled the towel off the waist of his own naked body and then lubed his hard huge black penis as he smoothly slid it inbetween Aidan's tight and smooth inner fleshly walls in pleasure as Aidan gasped out in a light moan of Jamal's entering of his tender white naked body.

Jamal began to explore the inside of Aidan as Aidan moaned out stutteringly in internal pleasure,Jamal's strong hands rubbing and caressing up and down his exposed shoulders and exposed back,Jamal's naked crotch drilling into Aidan's firm and round white naked buttocks in thrills of ecstasy.Jamal plunged himself deeper into Aidan's inner flesh walls as he gripped tightly to the back of Aidan's neck,Aidan crying in moans of pleasure,Aidan feeling Jamal's huge penis stabbing him inside as Jamal continued to thrust behind him.

The sound of naked flesh slapping against naked flesh filled the room as Jamal's long thick and hard male sex organ slammed deeply into Aidan's body from behind,Jamal's plump and round buttocks flexing a bit as he plunged back and forth and in and out of Aidan in hard strokes,his massive dark chocolate colored penis gliding back and forth inbetween Aidan's tight inner fleshly tunnel.

Jamal then easily turned Aidan over on his back as he stuffed Aidan's inner walls relentlessly in pleasure as he watched Aidan's facial expressions of pleasure,Aidan's facial expressions giving Jamal even more sexual kicks.Jamal's smooth and chocolate brown colored nude body moved up and down on Aidan's vanilla colored nude body as Aidan took him in fully and deeply in moans.

Jamal's hard penis throbbed in deep pleasure and near sexual eruption as he continued to plow deeply inside of Aidan on the leather sofa,Jamal and

Aidan's naked bodies fuming with heat.

Cum in me dude,cum all over me! Aidan ordered Jamal in deep lust as Jamal continued to push himself into him with hardcore thrusts of his exposed pelvis,Aidan wanting every bit of Jamal inside him and on him.

Jamal then lifted Aidan's leg to the side as he began to heavily ejaculate into him,Aidan's naked white body being flooded with Jamal's hot semen as jamal moaned out deeply in pleasure,Aidan then having an orgasm of his own as his heated loins exploded with an intense passion of pleasure.

Jamal then swiftly and smoothly turned Aidan back over on his stomach as he kept his hard penis connected to Aidan,Jamal then forcing Aidan's back to arch with his hand as he dug himself deeper into Aidan's round firm white and tight buttocks as it rose slightly to the air,Jamal shooting off a few more rounds of hot semen into Aidan's tight and very round buttocks in exhausted ecstasy,Aidan feeling himself being filled even more.

Aidan turned back over to face Jamal after their intense sexual completion,their eyes staring at each others raw nakedness in lust and passion as they caressed and kissed each other intimately on the leather sofa in their nudity.

Chapter 6

Three months had passed and Jamal and Aidan were both deeply in love and in lust with each other,Jamal giving Aidan a key to his house and Aidan giving Jamal a key to his house,Jamal's home becoming Aidan's home,and Aidan's home becoming Jamal's home,Jamal and Aidan even cracking jokes about how their child were to look if they were to have one every time they saw a biracial child,biracial children being an example of what couples of their nature could bring about.

It was a saturday night and Jamal and Aidan were relaxing silently side by side on a leather lounge sofa at the bathhouse in a private room,their bodies naked.

I love you dude,Aidan spoke warmly and silently to Jamal as he and Jamal held each other tightly.I love you too man,Jamal kissed Aidan softly and passionately on the lips as Aidan kissed him back with just as much passion.

Aidan and Jamal continued to kiss passionately until they heard someone knocking silently and repeatedly at their private room door,both their heads turning near the door with curiosity.

What's good man? Jamal spoke to the fully clothed man knocking at he and Aidan's private room door,his face confused.Ah,there's a woman outside who said she was here to see you,Jamal or Jamar,she's an older woman,black,and she seems kind of confused,i told her it might be best for her to stay outside and not see what goes on in here,the man spoke to Jamal as he stood at the private room doorway,the man being a parttime worker at the bathhouse.

Alright,dude im about to go see who this is,i be back,Jamal spoke to Aidan.Wait,im coming with you baby,Aidan spoke to Jamal as he accompanied Jamal down the hall of the bathhouse to see who it was exactly that came to pay him an unexpected visit.

Jamal swung open the back door of one of the secluded bathhouse exits and then received a shocking surprise,Jamal's mother Corraine was standing speechless as Jamal and Aidan swung open the door to the full view of their naked bodies standing side by side before her very eyes,Jamal and Aidan in shock at the unexpected sight of Corraine,Corraine who was Jamal's mother and Aidan's employee.

Jamal,Mr Aidan? Corraine spoke with a slight stutter,confusion on her face at the sight of her son and boss,together,both Jamal and Aidan then covering their exposed sex organs with their hands from Corraine's sight in modesty and slight embarrassment as their naked bodies stood closely side by side.

Ms Corraine,what are you doing here? Aidan spoke to Corraine with confusion on his handsome vanilla colored face,Aidan feeling guilty about having a sexual and romantic relationship with her very own son.Ma? Jamal then spoke to Corraine,shock,surprise,and confusion on his handsome chocolate colored face as well.

I came here looking for you,this man named Larry told me you came here a lot,i had showed up at your house to give you a surprise visit,and he told me you wasn't home when he happened to see me knocking on your door,and then he gave me the directions here,he told me i would be shocked by what i saw,Corraine explained to Jamal as Jamal listened to her carefully.

Jamal knew deep down that his distant neighbor Larry had wanted to expose his love life to Corraine,and he resented him for it,but he was also kind of relieved,he no longer wanted to keep secrets.

Are you gay baby? Corraine questioned Jamal warmly as she awaited his answer.Yea,im gay ma,and me and Aidan are partners,lovers,we been seeing each other before i came to visit you at work that day,im sorry if i disappointed you ma,but this is who i am,Jamal answered Corraine in honesty and fullness.

And i still love you baby,you're still my son,my baby,and i see you got yourself a swirl going on,oh Lord,im going have to bake a cake with one side chocolate and one side vanilla if yall was to ever get married,Corraine accepted a newly discovered part of Jamal she had never known of until now with an added innocent interracial joke as both Jamal and Aidan snickered in response.

Chapter 7

Five more months had passed and Jamal and Aidan were now married just as Corraine predicted they could be one day,their town being one of the progressive states that allowed same sex marriage.

Jamal and Aidan Celebrated their wedding with a small group of close friends and family and most of all Corraine,tho a few of Jamal's and Aidan's friends and family didn't attend the wedding because of both same sex and racial discrimination,tho Jamal and Aidan still enjoyed their big day,the day they announced their love for each other.

Jamal and Aidan celebrated their late night honeymoon at the bathhouse in a private room all to themselves alone after their wedding was over,their naked bodies embracing closely in nothing but the short white above knee length towels around the waists of their naked bodies as they kissed deeply and passionately near the moonlit window of the private room,their warm and moist lips intimately smooching,their smooth pecks and abs touching,the fabric of the short white towels around the waists of their naked bodies grazing,the warm flesh of their strong and toned thighs and knees and long legs meeting,and the thick shower shoes and flip flops on their feet colliding just as their lips continued to do all night long,and the night after that,and the night after that,and so on again and again.

The end

www.ingramcontent.com/pod-product-compliance
Lightning Source LLC
Chambersburg PA
CBHW020337290526
45785CB00005B/2064

9 781312 310957